W9-BCN-832

GPS and Computer Maps

JULIA J. QUINLAN

PowerKiDS
press.
New York

Published in 2012 by The Rosen Publishing Group, Inc.
29 East 21st Street, New York, NY 10010

First Edition

Editor: Amelie von Zumbusch
Book Design: Greg Tucker

Photo Credits: Cover, pp. 16, 17 iStockphoto/Thinkstock; p. 4 Jupiterimages/Comstock/Thinkstock; p. 5 Rayes/Digital Vision/Thinkstock; p. 6 (left) NASA/Space Frontiers/Getty Images; p. 6 (right) US Air Force photo/Senior Airman Cynthia Spalding; p. 7 Menahem Kahana/AFP/Getty Images; p. 8 Universal History Archive/Getty Images; p. 9 Dieter Spannknebel/Getty Images; pp. 10, 13, 14, 18 (left), 19 Shutterstock.com; p. 11 Comstock/Thinkstock; p. 12 © GeoAtlas; p. 15 Stockbyte/Thinkstock; p. 18 (right) by Greg Tucker; p. 20 Thinkstock Images/Comstock/Thinkstock; p. 21 National Atlas of the United States, http://nationalatlas.gov; p. 22 Jupiterimages/Creatas/Thinkstock.

Library of Congress Cataloging-in-Publication Data

Quinlan, Julia J.
 GPS and computer maps / by Julia J. Quinlan. — 1st ed.
     p. cm. — (How to use maps)
 Includes index.
 ISBN 978-1-4488-6159-0 (library binding) — ISBN 978-1-4488-6276-4 (pbk.) —
 ISBN 978-1-4488-6277-1 (6-pack)
 1. Global Positioning System—Juvenile literature. 2. Digital mapping—Juvenile literature. I. Title. II. Title: Global positioning system and computer maps.
 G109.5.Q56 2012
 910.285—dc23   8042
                          2011023951

Manufactured in the United States of America

CPSIA Compliance Information: Batch #WW12PK: For Further Information contact Rosen Publishing, New York, New York at 1-800-237-9932

Contents

Maps in Your Pocket

There are many kinds of maps. Some maps are on paper. Other maps are **electronic**. They can be on computers, on cell phones, and in cars. Many of these maps depend on the Global Positioning System, or GPS. GPS uses **satellites** to gather **information** about

Only certain cell phones show electronic maps. If you have the right kind of phone, though, you can use it to figure out where you are or where you need to go.

4

places. Satellites are spacecraft that circle Earth. To use GPS in a car, you need a GPS **receiver**. This is often just called a GPS.

Electronic maps are very useful. If you have one on your cell phone or in your car, you do not need to carry around a big map or **atlas**.

Having a GPS in your car makes it easy to find your way around. People with a GPS do not need to plan ahead as much when they take a trip.

The Global Positioning System

Maps have been used for thousands of years. GPS is fairly new, though. It was invented by the United States Department of Defense. Two **engineers** named Ivan Getting and Bradford Parkinson developed the **technology** for GPS.

Top: This rocket launched one of the early GPS satellites into space in May 1978.
Right: Members of the US military, such as these airmen, still depend on GPS today.

The Department of Defense sent the first GPS satellite into space in 1978. In 1993, it sent up its twenty-fourth satellite. The system was finally fully set up!

Before GPS, the Department of Defense had a satellite system that it used to guide **submarines**. It was not until 1993 that the government could use GPS on land. Until 2000, only the government used GPS. That year, it became available to everyone!

Scientists use GPS to study the movements of animals. This vulture has a tool on its back that lets scientists use GPS to track where the bird is.

How GPS Works

GPS satellites move at a speed of about 7,000 miles per hour (11,265 km/h). This drawing shows what one of these satellites looks like.

How does the information GPS satellites gather make its way to your car? The satellites send signals to the GPS receiver. The receiver can tell how long it takes for the signal to travel from the satellites. Based on how long the signal takes to get there, the receiver can tell how far it is from the satellites. This information lets the receiver figure out its location.

Even though there are more than 20 satellites, a receiver needs signals from only 4 to find its location. GPS satellites circle Earth twice each day. They are about 12,552 miles (20,200 km) above Earth.

Using signals from four different satellites makes it possible for a receiver to find its location more exactly.

Using Electronic Maps

Some cars come with built-in GPS receivers. People can also buy receivers and place them on their dashboards. Many GPS receivers will tell the driver directions out loud. For example, the receiver might say, "Turn right" or "Continue straight." This is helpful because it means that the driver does not have to stop and look at a map.

Cell phones that can show electronic maps on them have GPS receivers in them. They work the same way that a GPS in a car does.

Some cell phones receive GPS signals, too. The maps on these phones show where people holding the phones are with dots. The dots move as the people move. GPS on cell phones is helpful if you get lost!

The GPS is usually in the middle part of the dashboard in cars with a built-in GPS. This makes it easy for both the driver and the people riding in the car to see it.

Scale and Zoom

GPS maps and other electronic maps often let you zoom in and out of them. Zooming lets you see maps both close up and from far away. This is helpful if you are traveling from one place to another. You can zoom in

Physical Map of Pennsylvania

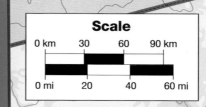

Scale

0 km	30	60	90 km

0 mi	20	40	60 mi

Delaware

Lackawanna

Susquehanna

Allentown

Delaware

Shenango
River Lake

Philadelphia

Raystown
Lake

HARRISBURG

Susquehanna

Pittsburgh

Ohio

Paper maps, such as this one, often have scales on them. The scale on this map is a bar scale.

close to see where you need to turn. You can also zoom out and see how far away you are from your **destination**.

On paper maps, you cannot zoom. Paper maps are only at one **scale**. This means they are always the same size. They either let you see an area up close or from far away.

To zoom in closer on this GPS map, people tap on the + sign on the screen. To zoom out and see more of the map, they touch the - sign.

Northeast to Wagner Rd

MARSHALL RD
GGER RD
WILMINGTON PIKE
E STROOP RD
INDIAN R
675

Turn In
0.1 mi

Arrival
6:28 PM

Menu

Symbols

The picture of a spoon and fork on this GPS map shows you the location of a restaurant. Can you guess what the picture of the gas pump means?

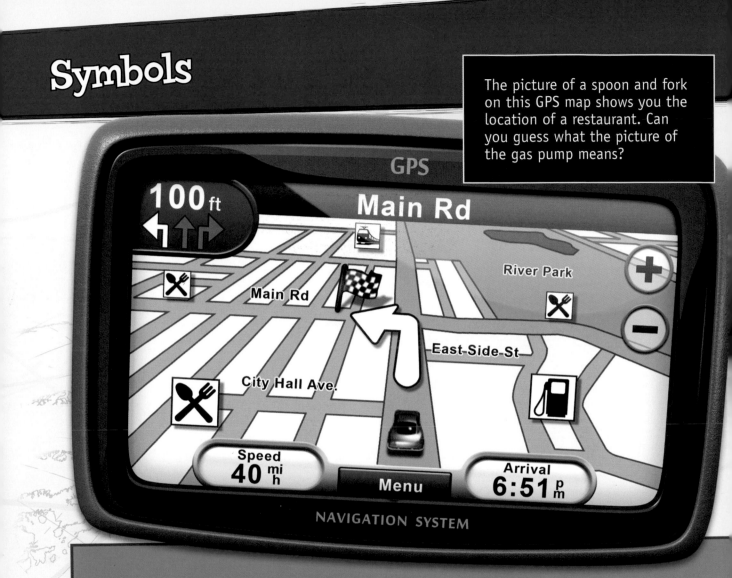

Electronic maps use **symbols**, just as paper maps do. Symbols are pictures that represent different places and things. An electronic map might have an "H" on it. An "H" usually shows you where a hospital is. Maps use lines to show roads and rivers. Maps of cities can have symbols for public transportation. They might have a picture of a train or bus to show where a stop is.

Maps can also have symbols for restaurants and stores. Symbols are used to show **landmarks**. Landmarks are important places in a town or city. A landmark could be a museum or city hall.

If your cell phone has GPS, you can use it to check what landmarks are nearby. You could discover new landmarks near your home this way!

Searching

Electronic maps are handy when you are looking for something. Many let you search for a place. You can type in what you are looking for and the electronic map will find it. If you are looking for a restaurant, you could type its name. The map will mark the restaurant with an arrow or other symbol. Electronic maps also let you search by

If you know the exact address of the place you are going, it is easy to search for it with a GPS.

typing in the address of the place you want to go. Some GPS receivers in cars even let you say what you are looking for out loud. That way people can find what they are looking for while they are driving.

A GPS is very helpful on family trips. It will give you directions to the place you want to go and help you find your way again if you take a wrong turn and get lost.

Getting Directions

Electronic maps make finding directions easy. All you have to do is type in the address of where you are and the address of the place where you want to go. The map will show you how to get there!

If you are using a GPS, you just have to put in your destination. It already knows where you are. Some cell phones work this way, too.

Top: Online maps are updated often. They may even know when a road is closed for construction. *Right*: You can look up electronic maps of some subway systems on the Internet.

Many electronic maps tell you how long your trip will take. Some even offer you different ways to get there. They might tell you how long it would take to walk, to drive, or to take public transportation.

You can find electronic maps online, too. While not all online maps use GPS, many do.

Maps Online

There are many Web sites that have electronic maps. Google has a site just for maps! It is called Google Maps. Google Maps gives directions. There is a **feature** called Street View that lets you see many places as if you were standing on the street.

Some Web sites give you directions that you can print out. This is a way to use electronic maps even if you do not have a GPS or cell phone that shows GPS maps.

MapQuest is another map Web site that many people use to get driving directions. You can print out directions from MapQuest and take them with you on a trip!

The United States Geological Survey and the Central Intelligence Agency sites have very good maps. Their maps do not give directions, but they are very useful and **accurate**.

Satellite View of the United States

This map of the lower 48 states of the United States was made from pictures taken from space. It comes from nationalatlas.gov, a Web site that supplies many kinds of maps.

The Future of Maps

Over time, electronic maps have become more and more accurate. They will become even more helpful as technology gets better. Someday we may have three-dimensional electronic maps. These would let us see faraway places as if we were actually there!

GPS and online maps are very handy tools. They make finding your way or finding where you are simple. They are easier to update than paper maps are, so they are less likely to be out of date. With one, you will never worry about getting lost!

Electronic maps have not been around for that long. However, they caught on quickly and are widely used today.

Glossary

accurate (A-kyuh-rut) Exactly right.

atlas (AT-lus) A book of maps.

destination (des-tih-NAY-shun) A place to which a person travels.

electronic (ih-lek-TRAH-nik) Having to do with computers.

engineers (en-juh-NEERZ) Masters at making and using technology.

feature (FEE-chur) A special part.

information (in-fer-MAY-shun) Knowledge or facts.

landmarks (LAND-marks) Buildings or places that are worth noticing.

receiver (rih-SEE-ver) A tool that picks up signals.

satellites (SA-tih-lyts) Spacecraft that circle Earth.

scale (SKAYL) The measurements on a map compared to actual measurements on Earth.

submarines (SUB-muh-reenz) Ships that are made to travel underwater.

symbols (SIM-bulz) Objects or pictures that stand for something else.

technology (tek-NAH-luh-jee) Advanced tools that help people do and make things.

Index

Web Sites

Due to the changing nature of Internet links, PowerKids Press has developed an online list of Web sites related to the subject of this book. This site is updated regularly. Please use this link to access the list:
www.powerkidslinks.com/maps/gps/

MAY   2012